Prehistoric Monsters

Prehistoric Monsters

Alfred Leutscher

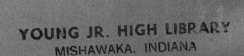

OCTOPUS

Contents

First published in 1979 by
Octopus Books Limited,
59 Grosvenor Street
London W1

ISBN 0 7064 0981 7

© 1979 Octopus Books Limited

Produced by Mandarin Publishers Limited
22a Westland Road, Quarry Bay, Hong Kong

Printed in Singapore

What is a Fossil?

I found my first fossil when I was a schoolboy on holiday at the sea-side. It was stuck to the cliff along the beach, and looked like some kind of tooth. I took it to a museum, and was told that it was the tooth of a shark which had died in the sea some 200 million years ago! What, then, was this tooth doing stuck in a cliff, how did it get there, and where was the rest of the skeleton? Also, what about its great age?

These are the sorts of questions which experts can find out by studying rocks and the fossils which they contain. Between them a geologist (jee-ol-o-jist) who studies rocks, and a palaeontologist (pay-lay-on-tol-o-jist) who studies fossils can bring ancient plants and animals back to life! We can learn what they looked like, when they lived, and how they behaved.

The Earth's crust in which fossils are buried is of three kinds. Some of the oldest and the hardest rocks are called igneous, meaning 'fire'. They come from inside the Earth whenever there is a volcanic eruption. The larva which erupts is very hot at first, so this destroys any plant or animal which gets caught in the larva flow. The larva then cools and hardens into an igneous rock. This forms into crystals, such as a rock called granite.

Fossils are rarely present in such rocks, except when a volcano erupts a cloud of ash. This can cover the ground and smother plants and animals. This is what happened to the citizens of Pompeii when Vesuvius erupted in AD 79. Their bodies were uncovered hundreds of years later – perfectly preserved.

A second kind of rock, called sedimentary, meaning 'laid down', is formed by erosion. Rocks are slowly worn away, or eroded, so that even a mountain may one day disappear. Wind, rain and frost break down the rocks, and particles are carried away by streams and rivers, ending up in a lake or a sea. In this way a mountain is worn away and a sea fills up. The sediment then hardens to become another layer of rock, which may be hundreds of feet thick and take millions of years to form.

Sedimentary rocks vary a lot in colour and hardness, depending on the particles they are made of. Sandstone is a hard and coarse sedimentary rock made of large grains. Very fine grains make a soft and smooth rock like chalk or clay.

A third rock, called metamorphic, meaning 'changed in form' is an altered rock usually close to a volcano or where there has been some movement in the Earth's crust. The tremendous heat or pressure changes the surrounding rocks into such material as slates and marbles. Fossils are rarely found in such rocks.

Fossils are best searched for in sedimentary rocks. When my shark died it sank to the sea-bed and was slowly covered with sediment washed down by rivers. The sea filled and hardened into a rock. Then, much later, another sea formed. Its waves beat against the shore and cliffs and so uncovered the rock in which my shark's tooth was buried.

Scientists have ways of telling the different ages of rocks, and when they were first formed. This tells the age of any fossils they contain, and when the plants or animals were alive. One method is called radio-active dating. Some igneous rocks contain radio-active materials whose parts, which are called atoms, gradually break down and change into other atoms. One of these is called uranium. Scientists know that its atoms change at a steady rate into those which make uranium-lead. By working out the amount of uranium still left in the rock, and the amount of uranium-lead which has formed, the age of the rock can be worked out. In this case, if half the amount or uranium has become lead, then the rock is about 4,500 million years old. This is called its 'half-life'.

Using this and other radio-active materials the various layers in the Earth's crust have all been dated, and the different forms of life they contain arranged into a kind of Earth calendar. These are shown on the chart (page 19). My shark's tooth came from a rock of the Jurassic Period, so it must have been 200 million years old!

Fossils from the Latin word 'fossilis' meaning dug up, are the remains or traces of any kind of prehistoric life which is preserved in the Earth's crust. This only happens by chance. Most dead plants or animals just rot away, or are eaten by scavengers, unless they are covered up soon after they die. This happens mostly when they die in water or soft mud and sand. Even so it is seldom complete, since the soft parts break up, leaving only the hard bones, teeth or shells. The skeleton of my shark had long since disappeared, as a shark's skeleton is made of a soft bone, called cartilage.

With all this knowledge of the Earth's crust, and how fossils are formed, it is possible to know where to look and what to expect. This saves a lot of time and money, especially when a party of scientists go off to collect fossils in faraway places difficult to reach, and where a lot of digging is necessary. You and I can look in places which are easy to reach, and where fossils are close to the surface. A sea-cliff, the face of a quarry, or in a chalk-pit are places where the Earth's crust has been uncovered, so little digging is needed. The fossil may be just waiting to be removed. As such places may be steep and a little dangerous it is important to remember the rules of a fossil hunter. First, be careful where you climb or tread. Second, never go alone but take a friend. He can then go for help if there is an accident. Tell the grown-ups where you are going, and always ask permission if you go onto private land.

Removing large fossils is really a job for a trained team of experts who have the proper tools and equipment. Small fossils like shells and teeth are what we can look for, and can be easily removed if the rock is soft. If it is hard then with a little care a fossil can be chipped away.

Below
A palaeontologist at work.

Above

This beautifully preserved skeleton of a fish, called *Eobothus*, is only 6 cm (2½ in) long but is clear in every detail. It is a kind of flatfish preserved in a piece of limestone taken from the hills at Monte Bolca in Italy where quarrying has been carried out for centuries. Eobothus was a flatfish, very closely related to modern flounders.

Above

Amber is a kind of hardened resin from a prehistoric tree. When soft and sticky it sometimes traps animals, seeds and twigs. This tiny insect is only 8 mm (⅜ in) long. Once hardened the amber lasts for millions of years. It is often washed up by the sea along the Baltic coast in Europe and is used for making ornaments and semi-precious necklaces.

Left

At a place called Rancho la Brea in Los Angeles, California, there was once a large number of lakes full of sticky tar. Rain which settled on top of the tar formed a death-trap for many animals. In this scene an elephant has come down to drink, and is trapped. Next, the sabre-tooth cat, hoping to kill and eat the elephant, is also caught. As they die the vulture in the tree will probably come down to feed. These are just three of an enormous number of animals, from insects to elephants, which have been trapped in this way. They were found when the tar was dug up and used for building roads.

Above

Even to-day there are times when severe droughts cause lakes to dry up. These fishes from the Triassic Period were caught and died in the mud which hardened into rock. It was once the bottom of a lake in South Africa which dried up comparatively recently. Similar species occurred in Triassic times in Arizona. They had strong teeth which they used for crushing moluscs and other invertebrates.

Above
This sea-urchin, called *Clypeus*, is about 7 cm (3 in) in diameter. It was found in Gloucestershire, England. When it died on the sea-bed the soft body and shell broke up, leaving a gap. This then filled up with a chalky sediment so as to make a cast of the urchin out of a limey rock. It was discovered many millions of years after the sea-urchins had become fossilized and is now, like many fossils on display in a museum.

Above
Ammonites are ancient cousins of the octopus and squid which swarmed in the seas of the Jurassic and Cretaceous Periods. All that is found today are the shells which covered their bodies. This shell of an ammonite called *Hoplites* has hardened into a mineral after so many millions of years. Ammonites get their name from the Egyptian ram-god Ammon, because their shells resemble that of a ram's-horn.

Left
This stuffed mammoth with its hair still on, in the Academy of Sciences in Leningrad, Russia, was found in this position by some trappers in Siberia. It was a young animal with a broken hip, blood in its chest, and food still between its teeth. It must have died suddenly from some accident, thousands of years ago, and was then frozen solid in the bitter cold of the Ice Age. The meat was so fresh that the trappers fed some to their dogs who gobbled it up.

Above
In many parts of the world have been found pieces of wood, even whole tree trunks which have become petrified, meaning 'turned into stone'. The wood has slowly dissolved away and been replaced with a mineral. Some wood is so perfectly preserved that the cell structure can still be seen. This is a view of the Petrified Forest in Arizona, U.S.A. Such forests are of great value to experts whose lives are devoted to studying prehistoric times.

Below

Where an animal has walked on soft ground it leaves footprints. If the mud then hardens into rock these are preserved. They could be anything from the tracks of a crab to the huge footprint of a dinosaur. Even such things as ripple marks made by waves on a beach, and marks of raindrops have been found in the rocks throughout the world.

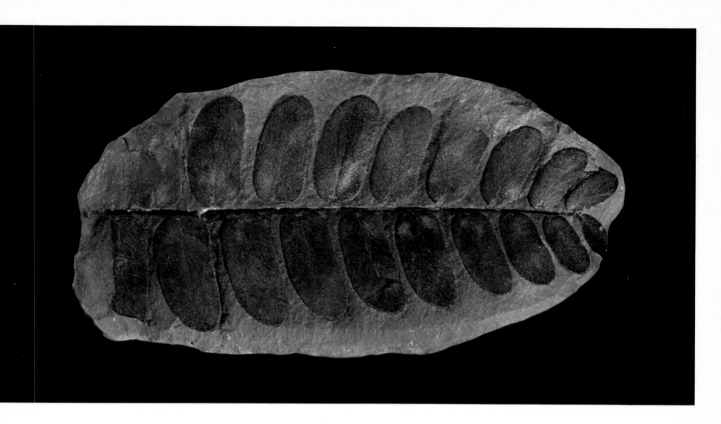

Above
Usually when an animal or plant dies it leaves no trace of its soft parts. Sometimes, however, a print of its skin leaves its mark. Leaf prints are quite common. This is the impression of a fern which was growing in a Coal Age forest.

Below
Worms which burrow in the ground or the sea-bed leave holes, and these are sometimes found as fossils.

Above
Each time the tide rises during storms the waves beat against the cliffs and gradually break off pieces which are further worn down to smooth pebbles, and finally into sand grains to form a beach. On some coasts the sea is eating into the land, and along others land is being added by the sea. In this way coastlines are being changed all the time at a very slow rate.

Below
Sand on the beach or in a desert is made of hard mineral particles. When this is blown about during a sandstorm it can wear down rocks, like sandpaper, and even damage buildings. Where it settles it can also cover up animals and plants which are unable to escape and therefore die. As millions of years pass these animals and plants become fossilized. Many fossils have been found in deserts.

Right
High up a mountain a stream is beginning the slow work of wearing away the rocks. Pieces are carried along to larger streams, then into rivers, and finally into the sea. In this way, slowly but surely, a whole mountain can disappear.

Below
Each time there is a shower of rain the water loosens the soil which is then washed into ditches and streams. If left to nature a pond, quarry or chalkpit may fill up to become dry land. This deserted claypit is already filling with rain-water, but soil is also being washed in from its bankside. Should it dry out, any fish in this pit may one day be caught and turn into fossils. Perhaps a fossil hunter of the future may find them.

Above

Molten lava gushing out of this volcano is pouring down the sides like a burning river. It covers the ground and will harden into an igneous rock. Sometimes black ash erupts and may fall into the sea. It gets washed on shore to form beaches of dark sand which are found in some volcanic areas.

Right

Granite is an igneous rock which forms crystals as it cools. The crystals reflect light as seen in this picture. Basalt is another igneous rock which forms below ground, and has even larger crystals.

Left
Layers of sedimentary rocks formed in ancient seas can be seen on the face of some cliffs and quarries. The layers may be broken or curved due to movements in the Earth's crust, and which have buckled under the enormous pressure.

Below
Some mountains, like the Cairngorms in the Scottish Highlands are formed of igneous rock. They wear down very slowly and are usually rounded in shape. Parts of the Highlands are 600 million years old.

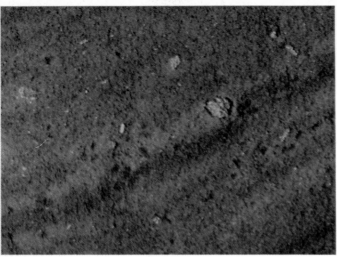

Above
This piece of sandstone is a hard and rough sedimentary rock. The separate pieces washed into some long lost sea have bound together to form the rock.

Right
This chart shows the different earth periods, as well as the life of the past, beginning with the small invertebrates of Paleozoic Era (at the bottom of the page) and ending with Man. As one period gave way to another, many forms of life were common to both periods; we have shown the major groups.

Below
The Colorado Canyon in America is a huge gash in the Earth's crust. In some places it is 1,580 m (5,280 ft) deep. As the river Colorado slowly cut its way into the crust it uncovered layers of rock up to 400 million years old.

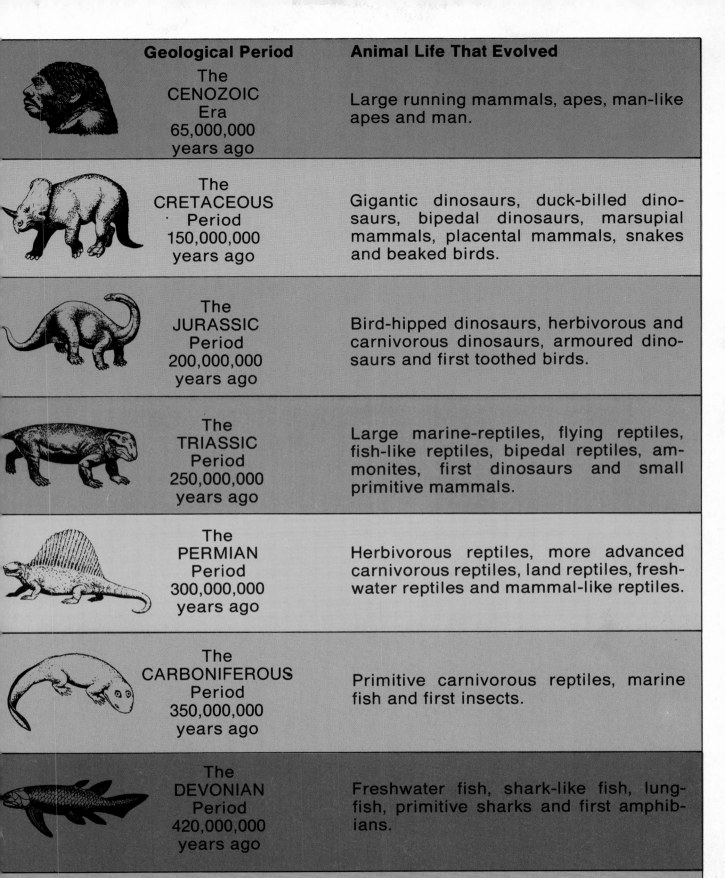

Geological Period	Animal Life That Evolved
The CENOZOIC Era 65,000,000 years ago	Large running mammals, apes, man-like apes and man.
The CRETACEOUS Period 150,000,000 years ago	Gigantic dinosaurs, duck-billed dinosaurs, bipedal dinosaurs, marsupial mammals, placental mammals, snakes and beaked birds.
The JURASSIC Period 200,000,000 years ago	Bird-hipped dinosaurs, herbivorous and carnivorous dinosaurs, armoured dinosaurs and first toothed birds.
The TRIASSIC Period 250,000,000 years ago	Large marine-reptiles, flying reptiles, fish-like reptiles, bipedal reptiles, ammonites, first dinosaurs and small primitive mammals.
The PERMIAN Period 300,000,000 years ago	Herbivorous reptiles, more advanced carnivorous reptiles, land reptiles, freshwater reptiles and mammal-like reptiles.
The CARBONIFEROUS Period 350,000,000 years ago	Primitive carnivorous reptiles, marine fish and first insects.
The DEVONIAN Period 420,000,000 years ago	Freshwater fish, shark-like fish, lungfish, primitive sharks and first amphibians.
The PALEOZOIC Era 600,000,000 years ago	Soft-bodied animals, corals, shelled-animals, echinoderms, sea scorpions, graptolites, brachiopods, trilobites and armoured jawless fish.

Above

Members of London's Natural History Museum are uncovering the remains of a woolly mammoth which was found in a claypit in Essex, England. When alive it wandered through the Thames valley during the Ice Age. It is being carefully boxed up so that the whole skeleton and tusks can be carried back to the Museum. It is now on exhibition in the Fossil gallery of the museum.

Below

Once in the museum a fossil skeleton is cleaned up, and the bones are treated with chemicals so that they do not break or wear away. If it is worth mounting then the bones are put together on a frame in the position they were in during life. This is a highly skilled job. The men and women who put the bones together are trained for a long time before they are allowed to work on a reconstruction.

Above and below
Fossil and model. If a fossil is preserved in good condition it may be possible to make a model of what it looked like when alive. This fish found in Italy lived among the coral reefs in a warm climate during the Eocene Period. The only thing we are unsure about is the colour.

How Life Began

The Bible story in Genesis, the first book of Moses, begins with these words – 'In the beginning God created heaven and earth . . .' It then goes on to say that He created all living things, including Man.

Is this true, or just a fairy story written by people with little knowledge of science and fossils? Or did life slowly evolve, or change, from simple beginnings to what we see around us today? Whichever is true, the Bible story or the story of Evolution and fossils, one important thing can be said. They both follow the same order, first when Earth was formed, then the appearance of plants, then animals, and finally man.

Gradually, scientists have come to realize that our Earth is far older than we used to think. In 1650 an Irish priest, Archbishop James Usher, worked out the age of the Earth from the Old Testament. He said it was born at nine o'clock on the morning of October 26th, in the year 4004 BC. Today scientists tell us that it was more like 4,600 million years ago! How it all started is not yet certain, but perhaps a cloud of hydrogen and star-dust broke away from the Milky Way, and the centre condensed into a baby sun. The spinning cloud around it broke into separate planets including our Earth. Today these planets still encircle the sun. As the sun contracted and its temperature rose, it produced sunlight. This swept away the gases between the planets so that Earth was bombarded with radio-activity. The Earth also contracted into a glowing ball, then slowly cooled. A crust formed around it, made of a hard igneous rock, called basalt. On this another rock, granite, formed into the continents which floated on the basalt-like icebergs in the sea of prehistoric times.

It is strange to think that we are living on huge, floating rafts. For countless years our restless Earth was full of upheavals. As the atmosphere cooled it brought rain. The rain fought with the hot Earth as lava poured from volcanoes. At first it turned into steam, but slowly the rain won. Rivers poured into the hollows between the rocks, forming lakes and seas. Minerals washed from the rocks turned the water salty.

It was somewhere along the ancient shores that scientists believe life began. How this was formed is still being worked out. We shall probably never know unless we can make it ourselves. It must have been a very minute kind of living soup from which all life started, since it could reproduce. This is the marvel of life, that it continues without a break.

Because it was so small and soft, this first life has left no traces, so there is a huge gap in time before examples of fossils turn up. The first appeared some 3,000 million years ago, in very ancient rocks in parts of Scotland, Norway and North America. They consist of layers of calcium carbonate forming rings as if something had grown there. Something very similar to this happens today with water plants, called stromatolites, meaning 'stony layers'. Tiny, blue-green algae build limey skeletons around themselves.

This took place in the Paleozoic Era ('ancient life'). Other signs of early life look like traces of fungus plants, worm burrows, and imprints of sponges and jellyfish. However, in those early days the rocks were so disturbed and worn that few good fossils have been found.

Much later larger animals began to appear, and by the time of the Cambrian Period, some 600 million years ago, we get much clearer pictures of ancient life. The seas were filled with seaweeds, but the land was almost bare of life. There were many kinds of sea animals, mostly of a small size, and with one thing in common. Although some had shells none possessed a backbone. We call them invertebrates. Many of their descendants still live today, such as corals and jellyfishes, sea-urchins, sponges, starfish, worms and various crabs. As yet there were no insects or spiders which live mostly on land.

Some of these early invertebrates are extinct, such as trilobites which got their name from the way in which their bodies were divided into three parts. Underneath they had jointed legs used for walking, burrowing or swimming. They looked somewhat like woodlice do today. Also extinct are the euryptarids (yew-rip-ter-ids) or sea-scorpions. They were among the largest sea animals in those early days, some growing up to 240 cm (8 ft) long.

Other invertebrates belonging to these early periods were the molluscs, such as various snails and clams, and especially the cephalopods (keff-al-o-pods), a name meaning 'head-foot'. The foot on which a snail crawls was divided into tentacles which surrounded the head, with a mouth in the middle. This is how modern squids and octopuses are built. The first cephalopods had shells. Some called ammonites had shells curled up like a sheep's horn. Others, the belemnites, had a pointed, cone-shaped shell. These are also mostly extinct. One survivor today is the Nautilus.

These are just a few of the invertebrates which have come and gone. Today an enormous number still survive, especially among the insects of the world.

Up until the Silurian Period, some 430 million years ago, the seas were full of small invertebrates. Then, in Scotland, a few of them, such as millepedes and scorpions, began to appear on land. More interesting, though, was the discovery, also in Scotland of a strange sea animal, about 25 cm (10 in) long, called *Jamoytius* (jam-oy-ee-shus). It had a simple backbone and is one of the first vertebrates.

Below
A fossilized trilobite.

Above
These beautiful ammonites are at least
75 million years old — probably older.
When they died, they sank to the bottom
of the ocean floor and gradually became
fossilized as millions of years passed.

Above
This fossil coral, called *Omphyma* (om-fee-ma) is one of the oldest kinds, which were shaped like a cone, and once thought to have been a plant. It was found at Dudley in Worcestershire, England.

Above
Syringopora is another coral found in Carboniferous limestone, and which helped to build up coral reefs and islands, like those found today in the Indian Ocean.

Above
Lonsdaleia found in Shropshire, England, is another coral found in Carboniferous limestone. Due to the flower-like shape of this coral it makes an attractive building stone when cut and polished.

Above
These curious shapes are fossils of a colony of animals, called graptolites, once believed to be plants. Tiny animals lived in cups attached to the stalks shown on these branches. They are called graptolites, meaning 'written in stone' because they look like pencil marks on this slaty rock.

Right
Sea-urchins get their name from the hedgehog, or urchin, because they are covered with spines. These are usually missing from a fossil called *Stereocidaris* (steer-ee-o-sigh-dare-is). This attractive sea-urchin was found in a chalk pit in Kent, England. It is about 5 cm (2 in) in diameter.

Above
Spirifer is the name for this brachiopod (brack-ee-o-pod). About 15 cm (6 in) wide it comes from a limestone rock in Britain. Because some brachiopods had shells like old Roman lamps these sea animals are sometimes called lampshells.

Below
This fine looking fossil of a starfish, called *Palasterina* comes from a Devonian rock in Germany. It looks almost alive as it crawls over the sea bottom, now turned into slate. It died some 500 million years ago during the Paleozoic Era when there was no vegetation.

Above
Another trilobite, this one from the Silurian Period, died on the sea-bed now turned into a hard, sandstone rock. It probably burrowed into the sand for safety.

Left
This enlarged model of the trilobite *Ceraurus* (ser-or-us) clearly shows how its shelly body is divided into three. It was 6 cm ($2\frac{1}{2}$ in) long and lived in the Ordovician Period. It was one of the larger types of trilobite and it had an extended head-shield and large antennae.

Above
Found in Ohio, U.S.A., this trilobite, called *Phacops* (fay-kops) died in a rolled-up position, and is sometimes called the 'woodlouse' trilobite, as some woodlice roll up for protection.

Above
Here is a finely preserved colony of crinoids (cry-noids) which look very much like flowers, but are actually cousins of the starfish which live on stalks. They waved about in the water of a Devonian sea, catching food. These are preserved in some very old slate found some time ago in Germany.

Right
Many worms which live in the sea build tubes in which they live. They have tentacles which they push out to catch their food, as these models show. They could be mistaken for underwater flowers. In front is a limpet-like mollusc, called *Scenella* (sen-ella). This is a scene from the Cambrian Period.

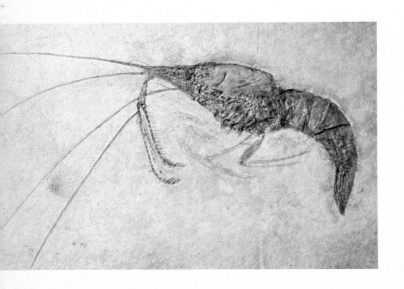

Left
This fine fossil of a crustacean, which includes crabs and lobsters, is a shrimp called *Aeger*. It was found in some Jurassic limestone at Solenhofen, Germany, a famous area for its fossils.

Above
Early Paleozic seas had lots of different types of plant life. Among them were these beautiful crinoids which remained almost unchanged throughout their history. This is a typical Silurian species which was found in Worcestershire in Britain.

Right
Crabs are called decapods, meaning 'ten feet' and all of them can be counted in this fossil which looks very much like a modern crab.

This is *Pterygotus* (ter-ee-go-tus) a large
sea-scorpion which grew up to 2½ m
(8 ft) long, and was one of the largest
invertebrates during the late Silurian and
early Devonian periods. It was a dangerous hunter, and even fishes were not safe.
Sea-scorpions, or Euryptarids are now
extinct. They only looked like scorpions
do today, but are not related to them.

Ancient waters must have teemed with
tiny animal life, as they do today, even
ponds and lakes. The smallest, one-
celled animals called Protozoa (the 'first
animals') are still with us today and
include the little *Amoeba* (a-mee-ba) or
Ghost Animalcule. It creeps about the
pond or ditch by pushing out parts of its
body in a ghost-like fashion.

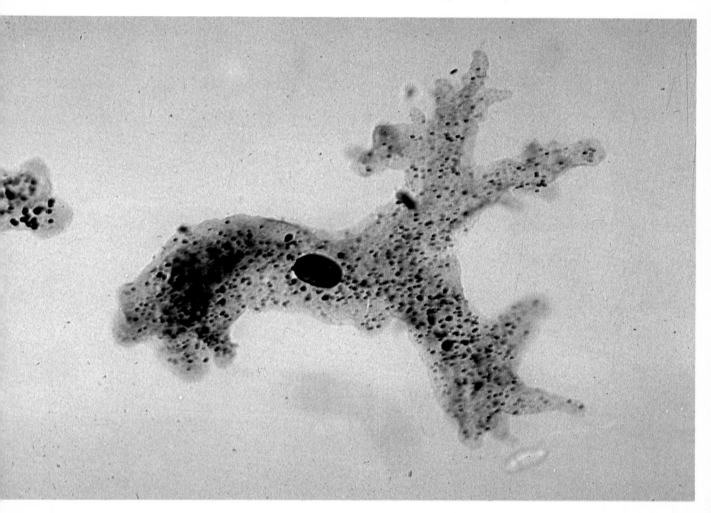

The Age of Fishes

Jamoytius was a small Silurian vertebrate, about 25 cm (10 in) long, and very similar to the lancelet, a small animal alive today. It lives in shallow sea around the coasts of Britain, California and Japan, and burrows into the sand. Much more advanced forms have been found which lived in the lakes and streams of the lower Devonian Period. They are called Ostracoderms or 'shell-skins'. As well as a backbone they had hard, bony plates covering their heads. Unlike fishes today they had no paired fins or jaws with teeth. Instead, mud and sand were sucked through the mouth and sifted for food. The eel-like lamprey is a special kind of ostracoderm. It lives in rivers and is a parasite since it attacks other fish. It clings to their bodies with its sucking mouth and feeds on flesh.

Apart from these early vertebrates further changes were taking place, and by the late Devonian there were four kinds of true fishes in the world. One group, the Placoderms or 'plated skins' were heavily armoured with a bony covering, and had jaws with teeth, also paired fins. Although they finally died out, some grew to enormous size, like *Dinichthys* (dye-nick-this) which sometimes grew to 10 m (30 ft) in length. Before they disappeared these placoderms gave rise to another group which is very much alive today – the sharks and rays. They include today's largest fish, the 13 m (40 ft) Whale shark. Such fishes have a soft skeleton made of cartilage bone which does not fossilize well, so that most shark fossils consist only of their teeth.

A third successful group is made up of most modern fishes. These are called Ray-fins. Their fins are spread over rows of bones rather like a fan. They are every-where – the herring in the sea, the trout in the river, and the stickleback in the pond. These are all true bony fishes. Among them, and very important to our story, are a number of bony fishes which appeared during the middle Devonian called Fringe-fins. In this case they had special fins growing on bony stalks, and could use them to push themselves through shallow water, even over land.

During the Devonian Period the weather was getting warmer, and many lakes and rivers were drying up. As a result many fishes were trapped on land and died, since they could not escape. To do so it was necessary to have lungs to breathe air, and limbs to walk on. A fish with gills and fins is helpless on land. This is where the Fringe-fins were lucky. They could struggle out of a dried-up lake and find another, still full of water. A good example is the Devonian Fringe-fin, called *Eusthenopteron* (yews-then-op-ter-on). Among these Fringe-fins were some fishes called Coelacanths (see-la-kanths). Up until 1939 it was thought that all coelacanths had become extinct. Then, some fishermen caught one off the coast of South Africa. It is very similar to the fossil kinds which lived as far back as the Devonian. These 'walking fish' are still with us today. They are real living fossils.

Also, of great interest, is another group called lungfishes, which still survive in the swamps and rivers of South America, Africa and Australia. Although they have gills for breathing under water, they also have a simple lung. This is very useful when the water dries up. During the dry season they burrow into the mud, and sleep until the rains fill the lake once more and they can swim again.

What does all this mean? All these changes – the appearance of Fringe-fins and lungfishes, meant that a way was open to leave the water world and come onto the land. To do so they had to have lungs to breathe, a backbone to support the body, and limbs to walk on. Between them the Devonian fishes had all three.

This great step onto the land was taking place during the late Devonian, so that by the next, Carboniferous Period, new life was appearing – the Amphibians.

Below
An artist's impression of prehistoric under-water life. This is during Triassic times when many of the early Paleozoic fish had died out and were replaced by others.

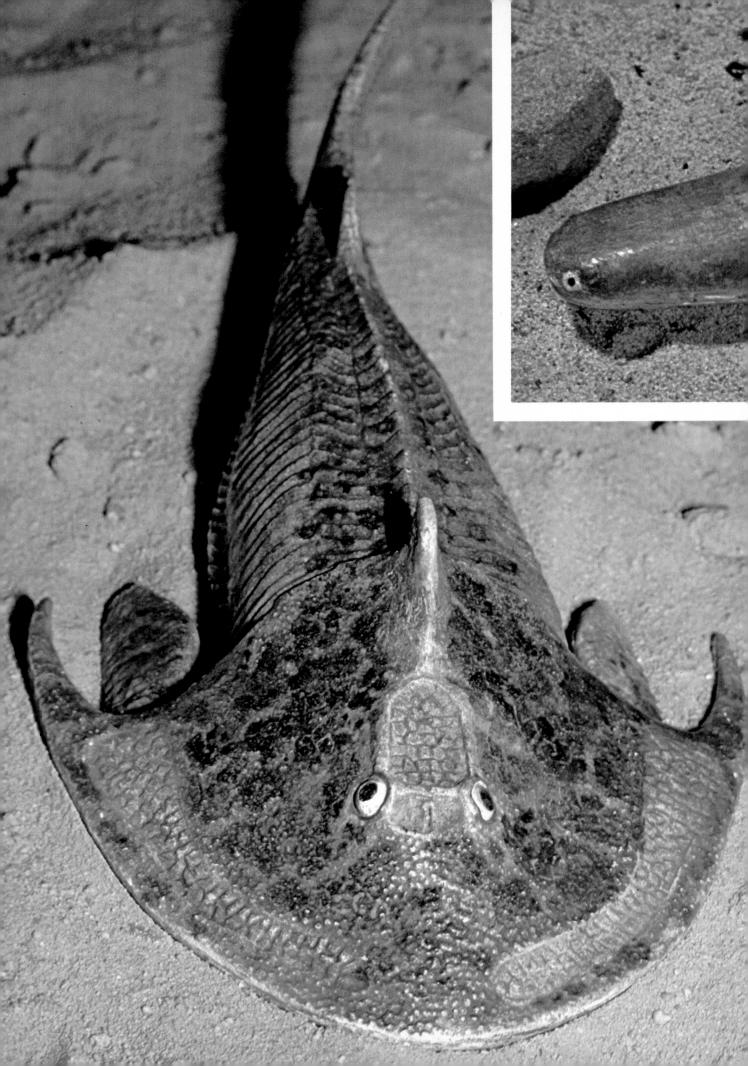

Above
Jamoytius from the Silurian Period was a primitive water vertebrate found in Scotland. It had a streamlined body. This model shows a skin fold along its back and sides, but no paired fins. The small mouth had no jaws or teeth.

Left
Cephalaspis (keff-a-las-pis) was an ostracoderm which lived in Devonian lakes, spending much of its time grubbing up food from the mud. Its head was covered with bony plates. It lived throughout Europe, Asia and America during Silurian times.

Above
A coelacanth, thought to be extinct, was discovered off the coast of Africa not so long ago. This is a model of a *Chondrosteus* which lived in Jurassic times – a close relation to the coelacanth.

This very fierce member of the placoderm fishes is called *Coccosteus*. Some placoderms reached a very large size, but all of them finally died out. This model shows the armour plating on its body. It had a broad, blunt head with rows of short, very sharp teeth in its wide mouth. It lived in the freshwater lakes of Europe and North America during the Upper Devonian.

Above
Bothreolepis is another placoderm, sometimes called the Box-fish because of its heavily armoured body. This model shows it on a sandy bottom. The two side 'arms' helped to give it balance.

Top
During Devonian times lungfishes were very common. This model of *Dipterus* is shown swimming normally in water. When the lake dried up it could burrow into the mud and use its simple lung to breathe with until the lake filled up again. There are still lungfishes alive today with the same habits. Notice the paired fins which have stalks similar to those of the other Fringe-fins of the time.

Above
This is a model of a very important fossil Fringe-fin, called *Eusthenopteron*, about 60 cm (2 ft) long. It is in the act of leaving a dried-up lake to find another, using its fins to walk on. This must have saved its life many times during droughts. It is on its way to becoming an amphibian. Eusthenopteron was one of the crossopterygian group of fish who adapted to the conditions.

Below
Among the very first true fishes were a number of small, shark-like kinds. This is *Acanthodes* and is modelled from a fossil found in Germany, and has a covering of thick scales.

Below

This scene is of a Devonian lake in a very dry countryside. It shows many different types of fishes. *Bothreolepis* (bottom right) is a placoderm fish. The fierce *Coccosteus* (bottom left), another placoderm, has just caught a fish. Far right is the lungfish *Dipterus*. Disappearing out of the picture left is the Fringe-fin *Eusthenopteron*.

This is one of the modern coelacanths, called *Latimeria*, which have been found off the coast of South Africa. They live in deep water and were not discovered until 1939. *Latimeria* clearly shows the fringe-like fins which were developed during the Devonian Period and were so helpful in escaping from dried-up lakes. It is a living relic of prehistory.

43

Right
Most modern salamanders live in North America. This one, found in Europe, is the famous Fire Salamander. People once believed that it could live in fire, and was deadly poisonous. In fact it is quite harmless.

Below
This is a model of *Ichthyostegia* (ik-thee-o-stee-jia), a primitive amphibian which lived and breathed on land, and walked about on its webbed feet. It used its tail for swimming just as newts do. It lived in the late Devonian, and was found in Greenland which in those days was as warm as the Tropics.

Below
This lake in a Coal Age forest shows the rotting vegetation and broken tree stumps which will slowly fill the lake and finally turn into coal which we use today. The fishes include the large placoderm, *Dinichthys* (behind the tree stump) also a primitive shark, *Pleuracanthus* (top right). A lungfish (bottom left) is searching for food along the bed of the lake.

Right
There were many dragonflies, like this one called *Meganeura* (meg-an-your-a) living in the Coal Age forests, and were the largest insects. This giant had wings nearly 1 m (3 ft) across! The fast movement of the wings must have created a tremendous noise as the dragonflies flew over the prehistoric forests.

Invasion of the Land

It is not quite certain how amphibians evolved into reptiles, but there is one difference we do know, apart from the way their different skeletons are built. Whereas amphibians lay eggs in water, reptiles can lay them on land. They were the first vertebrates to do so, simply by covering their eggs with a shell. This means that the young, instead of growing up in water, can grow inside a kind of 'private pond'. Inside the egg-shell is water, the albumen, and food, the yolk. The baby reptile finally hatches with lungs and legs already developed and can start life on land. There is no need for a water stage. This great step must have taken place sometime during the Permian Period, and started the greatest invasion the world has ever known – the invasion of the land.

Apart from laying shell-eggs, and having stronger skeletons, reptiles are protected with a scaly covering, just like the snakes, lizards and crocodiles of today. The tortoise has an even stronger, bony shell. This means that they can stand more sunlight, and will sometimes bask for hours, just lying about, something an amphibian can never do with safety. Reptiles can even live in dry and hot deserts.

Being cold-blooded, reptiles get much of their warmth from their surroundings. In countries with cold winters they hibernate, and most of them live in the Tropics. Unlike warm-blooded mammals their brains are poorly developed. The largest modern reptile, the crocodile, has a brain no bigger than a man's thumb.

Such are today's reptiles. The first to appear during the Permian are called Theraspids, or Mammal-like reptiles. In some ways they resembled mammals by holding their bodies well off the ground. Most reptiles tend to crawl about on their bellies, with their legs held at the side. Also, theraspids had teeth of different shapes, some for chewing food, and others for tearing up meat. True reptiles have sharp, curved teeth, all alike, and only used for catching and holding prey which is swallowed whole, or just torn up in lumps. Mammals usually chew their food before swallowing.

Large numbers of theraspids have been found in South Africa. These include a clumsy plant-eater, called *Pareiosaurus* (par-aye-o-sore-us) and a hunter called *Cynognathus* (sigh-no-gnay-thus). Another very strange looking reptile was *Dimetrodon* (dye-met-row-don) which had a kind of sail on its back.

Herds of theraspid reptiles dominated the Permian Period. It was a time of great changes. Volcanoes were in action, and there was even an ice age in the southern hemisphere. Seas were drying up in the warm areas, and becoming more salty. Ammonites and cephalopods were common, but trilobites and sea-scorpions were dying out. So were many amphibians which clung to the edges of lakes and rivers. Only the larger ones, like *Seymouria*, stood much chance against the reptiles.

But then it became the turn of the theraspids to make way for a new group, reptiles called Thecodonts (thee-ko-donts). These were for the most part much smaller, but far more active. They ran about on their hind legs. Lively and swift they slowly took the place of the more clumsy theraspids. It is quite possible that they were even warm-blooded. One of these is called *Euparkeria* (yew-par-keer-ia).

This was a time when two important steps took place among reptiles. Most theraspids died out, except for one successful group which eventually gave rise to mammals. We shall meet them later. On the other hand the thecodonts developed in another direction – into the dinosaurs and to the pterosaurs.

Below
Some amphibians like this giant salamander *Eryops*, grew quite large. It was $2\frac{1}{2}$ m ($7\frac{1}{2}$ ft) long. Being large and heavy it probably dragged itself along slowly, and stayed close to the waterside. It was found in America but it was by no means common and has only been found there.

Previous page
This fossil skeleton of *Seymouria* is about 60 cm (2 ft) long. It is a mixture of amphibian and reptile. Since no eggs have been found with these remains we cannot be sure that it was a proper reptile, even though it lived entirely on land. *Seymouria* was found in Texas, U.S.A.

Above
Cynognathus, meaning 'dog jaw', was a hunting theraspid with dog-like teeth which are shown in this skull found in southern Africa. It is a stepping stone towards the later mammals.

Right
This clumsy looking *Pareiosaurus* roamed about in herds rather like the buffalo on the American prairies. It was 3½ m (12 ft) long but lived more in swampy areas, feeding on soft plants.

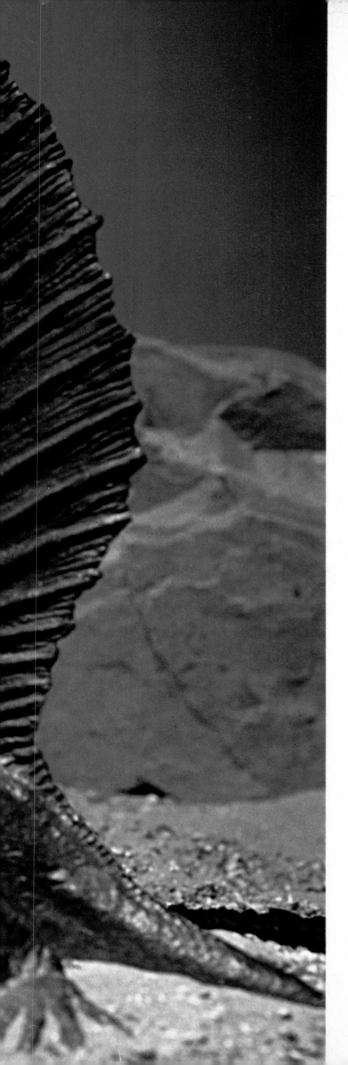

Left
The strange-looking *Dimetrodon* had a large fin on its back, supported by rows of bones. It is sometimes called the sail-back or ship lizard. The sail had nothing to do with ships or with swimming but probably helped to get rid of heat and cool its body. Dogs use their tongues when they pant, for the same reason. *Dimetrodon* was a hunter, about 4 m (12 ft) in size.

Overleaf
This little thecodont reptile, called *Euparkeria*, was only 1½ m (5 ft) tall, and ran about on its hind legs. The tail made a useful balance. Some scientists think that *Euparkeria* and similar two-legged reptiles were the ancestors of the dinosaurs, and may well have been warm-blooded. They existed during the Triassic Period, about 250,000,000 years ago.

The World of Dinosaurs

When we look at a mounted skeleton of a dinosaur in a museum, it is hard to believe that such strange looking giants ever lived. And yet if we saw an elephant or a giraffe for the first time they would seem just as odd. Bones cannot lie, and when the first huge bones and footprints were found they caused a sensation. Richard Owen, who was Director of the Natural History Museum in London, and a fossil expert, called them Dinosaurs (dye-no-sores) meaning 'terrible lizards'.

Even so, when more was known about them, they were thought to be cold-blooded and rather stupid reptiles, with clumsy bodies and tiny brains. In those days only a few fossils had been found, but today we know a lot more about them. Using modern scientific methods they have been examined in great detail. Bones have been carefully studied, and the result comes as a surprise. Far from being cold-blooded and awkward they could well have been warm-blooded and quite lively animals. They were no longer reptiles but a totally new group of vertebrates. Their tiny ancestor, *Euparkeria*, had really started something!

Among the very first remains of dinosaurs to be discovered were some teeth. They were picked up by the roadside by Mrs Mantell, a doctor's wife living at Lewes in Sussex, England. Being interested in fossils Dr Mantell searched in a nearby quarry and found further remains. Because these teeth looked very similar to those of a group of American lizards called iguanas, he named his dinosaur *Iguanodon* (ig-yew-are-no-don), the 'iguana tooth'. Later on an almost complete skeleton was found in the cliffs of the Isle of Wight, England. Then, in Belgium, some thirty skeletons were uncovered in a coal mine. They must have fallen to their deaths.

Discoveries like this started a world-wide search for further dinosaurs, especially in America. Two wealthy collectors, Richard Cope and Othniel Marsh, organised search parties to find and dig up skeletons wherever they might occur. The best hunting grounds were in the area where the Cretaceous rocks meet the Jurassic rocks, especially in the mid-western states of Wyoming, Colorado and Utah. Jealous of one another Marsh and Cope would try to beat each other by trying to get at the fossils before the other, even sending out spies! This became known as the Battle of the Bones, and started in 1877. As a result a splendid collection of all kinds of dinosaurs can now be seen in many museums, especially in America.

Dinosaurs were at their greatest during the Jurassic and Cretaceous Periods. The Jurassic was a warm time of rich plant life, consisting of evergreens such as tree-ferns, conifers and plants called cycads. They kept their leaves all year round in a kind of everlasting summer. Food was plentiful, and enormous quantities must have been eaten by the giant plant eaters. One of these, called *Stegosaurus* weighed up to 10 tons. Even greater was the popular *Brontosaurus* (also called *Apatosaurus*). With its long neck it could reach high into the branches of trees for the best leaves, as a giraffe does. This would only have been possible if it were warm-blooded and had strong enough muscles to hold up its body and neck. On the other hand, were it cold-blooded then it may have lived mostly in shallow lakes so that the water could support its weight. In that case the long neck would have been a useful kind of periscope, and could reach out to gather water plants. Scientists are still not decided which kind of life is correct. At least, its name is well suited. *Brontosaurus* means 'thunder lizard', and the ground must have trembled as it walked past. One thing we shall never know is the kinds of noises these giants made, but they must have sounded frightening.

Then, in the following Cretaceous Period, dinosaurs of a different kind appeared. There was the horned *Triceratops* (try-ker-a-tops), and its close cousin *Styracosaurus* (sty-rak-o-sore-rus); both were plant eaters which were heavily armed with horns and a bony shield behind the neck. They had to protect themselves from such hunters as the mighty *Tyrannosaurus* (tie-ran-o-sore-us). We can imagine the tremendous battles which went on when they met. Occasional fossil bones have been found with teeth marks, even two skeletons locked together in what looks like a death struggle.

Among the smaller kinds of dinosaurs were some which resembled large birds, but without feathers and having arms. One of these is called *Struthionomus* (stroo-thee-on-o-mus) meaning 'ostrich mimic'. In fact, when its legs were first examined it was mistaken for a bird. It was a swift runner, and used its clawed feet for digging up roots and eggs. Its long neck and beaked mouth could reach up to feed on tall plants. These are just a few examples of a truly remarkable group of prehistoric animals about which we still have a lot to learn. If the new idea that they were really warm-blooded and active is true, then perhaps it is just as well that we were not alive in those days!

Below
These are eggs of *Protoceratops* from which the babies are hatching. Found in the Gobi Desert, Mongolia, the eggs were so well preserved that the young inside could be reconstructed, making it possible to build this model. Had these babies lived they would have been around 80 million years ago in the early part of the Cretaceous Period. The parents were small, about 2 m (6 ft) long, and had a shield but no horns.

Above
Stegosaurs were among the oddest looking dinosaurs. They had double rows of pointed protective armour plates along their backs. It was probably quite a gentle species and its armour would have made it difficult for its predators.

Above
This hunting *Ceratosaurus* was found near Canyon City in Colorado, America. It was about 7 m (22 ft) and must have been a powerful enemy. It has just killed its victim, probably a *Brontosaurus*, with its large claws and sharp teeth.

Left
Brontosaurus was a Jurassic dinosaur, up to 30 m (98 ft) long, and weighed 30 tons. It was a harmless vegetarian and spent much of its time in swamp land. It was one of the first dinosaurs to have two brains, one in its head and one in the hip region. The second one probably helped to control its tail and its main brain in its head was no larger than a kitten's.

Left
This picture shows a pair of *Allosaurus* tearing off meat from their prey. They were very similar in build to *Cerato-saurus*. In the background is an armoured dinosaur, called *Ankylosaurus* (an-kye-low-sore-us). The plants are giant horse-tails which were common during the Jurassic Period, 200,000,000 years ago.

Below
This scene is of a Jurassic sea and shows a number of bony fishes, corals, molluscs and ammonites. This was the time when sea reptiles like ichthyosaurs and plesiosaurs existed, who lived off the weaker forms of life in the sea just as the larger fish and mammals today survive by hunting smaller species.

Triceratops the 'three-horned face' had a large, bony shield over its neck, a useful protection against enemies. It could face danger by lowering its head, like an antelope does when attacked by a lion, and use its horns to drive off its foe. Like many other dinosaurs it had a 'second brain' in its hip region. *Triceratops* measured 8 m (25 ft), and so far has only been found in America.

Above

Tyrannosaurus rex, the 'king of the tyrant lizards' well deserves its name. This mightiest of dinosaur hunters must have been a kind of lord of the jungle, as the tiger is today. It measured over 15 m (46 ft) from nose to tail, and stood 6 m (18 ft) off the ground. If it was alive today it could have peered through the upper windows of a modern house. Its powerful hind claws were used to grip its prey, in the way a bird-of-prey does. The very short arms, and six-inch teeth used to tear it apart. The arms were not much use as they could not even reach the mouth. However, they could have helped to push it upright from the ground, after it had been lying down.

Below
This is *Styracosaurus*, another horned dinosaur and a cousin of *Triceratops*. In addition to its horn it had a row of sharp spikes in place of a neck shield. It was also found in North America. The spikes evolved from earlier frills and were used as a means of defence when fighting off other dinosaurs which would try to attack it — they were probably very effective.

Overleaf
These two Duckbills, called *Anatosaurus*, were alive in North America shortly after *Iguanodon* which lived in Europe. These models show their flat mouths which contained as many as 2,000 teeth! They were used for crushing plant food. The toes were webbed, and the tail flattened, so they were probably good swimmers. Many fossils have been found in the western states of America.

Right
The 'ostrich mimic' *Struthiomimus* had a slender body and ostrich-like legs for swift running. Its long neck with a toothless, horny beak reached into the trees to gather food. It stood 3 m (9 ft) high.

Below
During the Cretaceous Period, a word meaning chalk, there were warm and shallow seas which slowly filled up with the minute shells of tiny sea animals. This has hardened into the familiar white rock of the chalk downs of England. The chalk shows up along chalk cliffs. It took about 30,000 years to build up a one-foot layer of chalk. The cliffs of Dover took over 2 million years to form. This scene shows a number of bony fishes which by then were becoming more common. Fringe-fins were dying out, so were the coelacanths, although one can be seen in the background, on the left of the picture. A pterosaur is flying over the sea.

Conquest of the Sea and Air

In the south of England, on the Dorset Jurassic cliffs rich in fossils. It was there that Mary Anning, a fossil collector found the first ichthyosaur when she was only 12 years old. Then, at 22, she discovered the very first plesiosaur. It is on exhibition in London's Natural History Museum.

Mary's first discovery was in 1811. Much earlier, in 1776, an enormous skull with jaw bones was found in a chalk pit in south Holland. The finder took it to the town of Maastricht. News soon spread, with all sorts of stories about the discovery of a giant 'sea-serpent'. At that time the French were at war with Holland. When the Dutch town fell to the French, their general ordered his soldiers to capture the 'serpent' which was later taken to the museum in Paris. Examined by experts it turned out to be a sea reptile, not a whale or some kind of dragon or Loch Ness monster. It is called *Mosasaurus* the 'lizard of the Meuse' after the name of the river Meuse.

Similar sea reptiles have also been found in North America, some as long as 16 m (50 ft). Although sea-dwellers, the name mosasaur is a good one as they are early relatives of lizards.

The old seas of the Jurassic and Cretaceous were dominated by these sea 'dragons' as they were once called. Meanwhile another conquest was made in the air, long before there were any birds. Puzzling fossils of delicate bones were found in Germany with what looked like long wing-like arms. At first they were thought to be swimmers, using their wings as penguins do. Then, the French scientist Georges Cuvier examined a skeleton, and said it must have been able to fly. He called it *Pterodactylus* (tero-dak-tie-lus), meaning 'wing-finger', because one of the fingers was extremely long. The skin of the wing stretched along the arm and as far as the tip of this long finger. Such a wing would seem hardly strong enough to fly with. And yet, as with dinosaurs, the new idea is that the smaller kinds of pterosaurs (as the whole group are called) were warm-blooded and active. Some were no bigger than a sparrow.

Some remains of pterosaurs have markings on them which might have been hair. Were they, in fact, warm-blooded and furry animals? Their skulls show that they had good brains, and may well have looked after their young, as birds do.

Apart from smaller pterosaurs there were also some giants, like *Pteranodon* (ter-an-o-don) found in Kansas, U.S.A. Its wings stretched 8 m (25 ft) across. Whether it was too heavy to fly is not certain. Perhaps it just glided over the surface of the sea, like an albatross.

Where were the birds all this time? Up until 1860 there was no signs of any fossils showing feathers. Then, in the German quarry at Solenhofen, where the sea reptiles and pterosaurs were so common, a piece of limestone was uncovered, on which appeared a clear imprint of a feather. So, what was a bird doing in this graveyard of reptiles? Soon after that, a beautiful skeleton, but without its head, was found in the same area. About the size of a crow it looked very bird-like. It was clearly marked with feathers. On the other hand it had arms with fingers and claws, and a long tail which is never found in modern birds. Had it been covered in scales it would have looked like a lizard. This precious fossil is on show in the museum in London. Then, another skeleton turned up, this time with a head. Its jaws were full of teeth! Known as *Archaeopteryx*, the 'ancient wing', this odd-looking creature has been described as 'a reptile dressed up as a bird'. Since it was feathered *Archaeopteryx* was almost certainly warm-blooded. Its feathers were meant to keep it warm, not to fly with. Flying came much later. It lived mostly on the ground but could also climb the trees.

After careful study of its remains, *Archaeopteryx* compares most nearly to a small dinosaur found in the same quarry. It is called *Compsognathus* (kom-so-gnay-thus), a small, running dinosaur about 60 cm (2 ft) tall. It does seem as if *Archaeopteryx* is related to the dinosaurs, and is the true forefather of all modern birds.

All these discoveries have given us some idea of a strange but exciting world of animals, during which there were no humans. From the Triassic to the Cretaceous Periods it lasted for some 120 million years. Then, something went wrong. Dinosaurs, ichthyosaurs, plesiosaurs, and many others, all died out, leaving behind only their remains for us to find. It is still not clear what happened. Maybe a change of climate and a shortage of food killed them off. Perhaps there was some kind of killing disease, or maybe they just wore themselves out. Or there could have been a tremendous explosion in the heavens, due to a bursting star. The deadly radiation would have killed off most of the larger animals, since they could not hide. One interesting discovery is that the eggs which were being laid at the time of this disaster were very thin-shelled, so maybe the young never hatched. One day we shall know.

Whatever happened a new life was dawning by the end of the Cretaceous Period. New kinds of plants which grow flowers, as they do today, were appearing, and there were now seasons of winter and summer. Also a new age of animals was about to begin – the Age of Mammals.

Below
Pteranodon is one of the largest pterosaurs, and lived during the late Cretaceous Period. It had a toothless beak, a bony crest on its head, and a short tail. It was probably not strong enough to fly. Instead, it glided over the sea, looking for fish near the surface. Like birds, pterosaurs had hollow bones.

Left
This skeleton of *Rhamphorhynchus* (ram-for-rin-kus), a small pterosaur about 60 cm (2 ft) long, shows the very long fourth finger on each arm over which the wings were stretched. Being rather small it is thought that it could fly quite well, and was warm-blooded and hairy. The claws of its feet were used to cling to trees and cliffs, upside down like a bat. Most remains of pterosaurs, like those found in the Solenhofen quarries, in Germany, were close to what used to be lakes and sea. They probably hunted fish.

Below
This is a model of *Rhamphorhynchus* in flight, with a fish it has caught. It shows clearly the long fourth fingers which support its wings. Mary Anning who found the first ichthyosaur and plesiosaur at Lyme Regis in England, also found the first British pterosaur.

Above
This ichthyosaur is called *Ophthalmosaurus* (off-thal-mow-sore-us) and is about 3 m (9 ft) long. It looks very fish-like but was a true sea reptile. Streamlined and very swift it could easily catch fish with its sharp teeth.

Below
This beautiful fossil of an ichthyosaur was found in the Solenhofen quarry in Germany. It not only shows the skeleton but also the outline of its body. This clearly shows the fin on its back, the fish-like tail, and swimming paddles.

Left

This is a model of perhaps the most famous of all fossils ever discovered – the first feathered animal *Archaeopteryx*. It is now believed to be a feathered dinosaur which lived during the Jurassic Period, and is a link between reptiles and birds. Its wing feathers are spread over its arms which end in fingers with claws. The jaws have teeth, and it had a long, feathered tail. It probably could not fly well, but could climb.

Right

This model of a nothosaur (know-thow-sore) is based on a fossil from Triassic rocks found in Austria. It is about 23 cm (9 in) long. Nothosaurs were among the first sea reptiles whose arms and legs were not yet closed into paddles. Probably they could walk on land as well as swim.

Below

A skull of a pliosaur, a cousin of the plesiosaurs, which shows the sharp and curved teeth used by these sea reptiles for catching fish. Notice also the opening of the nostril, which shows that, unlike fish, they breathed air.

Mammals Take Over

As we have already seen, it was during the Triassic Period, at about the same time as the little thecodonts were evolving into dinosaurs, that most of the theraspid reptiles were dying out. A few, however, stayed on, and it is these that changed into mammals. At first these mammals were very small, and so far we have very few fossils to go on. The first discoveries were some minute teeth, little more than 1 mm long, found in Wales. Then, in 1948 a small skull was unearthed in China. More skulls turned up in Africa, in 1962 and 1966. These were only about 2 cm ($\frac{3}{4}$ in) long. It is no wonder that they have taken so long to find. And why should they be so important? And how do we know they belonged to mammals and not reptiles?

Like us, mammals only grow two sets of teeth, the baby milk teeth, then proper teeth as adults. Reptiles on the other hand continually grow new teeth as the old ones drop out. Also, they vary in size. Among these tiny mammal discoveries only two kinds were found, milk and permanent teeth.

From these flimsy remains we get a picture of active, warm-blooded and furry midgets resembling shrews.

The next period after the Cretaceous is called the Eocene, or Dawn Period. Here we get plenty of fossils to study, and can build up a picture of what life looked like in this world of mammals.

At first they were rather small. One of these was a group of primitive horses. *Hyracotherium* (hie-rak-o-theer-i-um) lived in America, and *Eohippus* (ee-o-hip-pus) the 'dawn horse' in Europe. They were no bigger than a fox-terrier. *Eohippus* walked on separate toes, four in front and three behind. It lived in tropical forests full of trees and undergrowth, where it had plenty of hiding places from enemies. Its teeth were shallow, since it fed on soft leaves. Its toes could spread out when it walked on soft ground.

That was only a beginning. Many more horses have been found at later periods, getting bigger every time. They rose higher and higher onto their toes, so that horses today have only one toe left on each leg. This change had a lot to do with the new surroundings in which they lived. Modern wild horses, which include wild asses and zebras, live in open country not jungles. There is nowhere to hide, so strength and speed is the only way to escape from danger. Also, modern horses have much stronger teeth for eating grass rather than leaves, and this takes a lot more work to chew.

The story of horses is now well known and shows very well how animal life changes with its surroundings. Charles Darwin, the great English naturalist called this the 'survival of the fittest'. By this he meant that an animal or plant, if it is to live successfully, must fit in with its surroundings, like a squirrel built for climbing and living in trees, or a fish for swimming and breathing in water.

Another well-known story is about elephants. One of the earliest was a small elephant, called *Moeritherium* (mer-i-theer-i-um) which was found in Egypt. It was no bigger than a pig. Today the elephant is our largest land mammal. So over the centuries elephants must have become bigger and bigger.

One of the most interesting mammals of the Eocene Period is a small tree-dweller, called a Tarsioid. It belongs to the lemur family. Tarsiers are still living today in the jungles of the Far East. They have hands, like we do, and large eyes in front of their faces for telling distance when they jump. This is so with all mammals called Primates, which started as tiny mammals, then developed into monkeys, then apes, and finally Man.

It was during the time when apes existed that some of them started to develop human features. In 1948, a skull of a small tree-ape was found on Rusinga island in Lake Victoria, Africa. Called *Proconsul* it had human-like teeth which look different from ape teeth.

From Africa early man slowly wandered into Asia and Europe. Two further discoveries look even more human, one from Peking in China and the other from Java (now Indonesia). These were Stone Age hunters, called *Homo erectus*, meaning 'upright man' who lived about half a million years ago. They were the first to make use of fire. These early ancestors had to face many enemies, such as the lion and the sabre-tooth cat.

On reaching South America early man met still further giants, such as the giant ground sloth, *Megatherium* (meg-a-theer--um) and the giant armadillo *Mylodon* (my-lo-don). Some dried skin of a giant sloth was even found in a cave in Patagonia where it may have been trapped and killed, even eaten, by the hunters.

Long before Man arrived in America other huge beasts roamed the prairies, like the bison of today. Some were found in the land of the Sioux Indians, who called them 'thunder beasts'. Othniel Marsh the dinosaur hunter called one of them *Brontotherium* the 'thunder beast'.

Since mammals are evolved from reptiles, did they ever lay eggs? This could well be so, since such mammals still exist today. In Australia there is a strange looking mammal, the *Platypus*, meaning 'flat-feet', which lives along the banks of streams and lakes in eastern parts of Australia. It has webbed feet and swims well. It also digs a tunnel in which eggs are laid. These hatch into babies which then feed on their mother's milk. The other egg-layer is the *Echidna* or Spiny anteater which carries the eggs inside a pouch. It is covered in sharp spines and has strong claws.

There are a number of different kinds of marsupials living in Australia, including the attractive 'teddy-bear' called the Koala. There is also a marsupial mole, cat and wolf and, of course, the kangaroo.

Our story started those 3,000 million years ago with the tiny plants preserved in the ancient rocks. What will come next?

Below
The earliest mammals appeared in late Triassic and early Jurassic times and appear to have descended from the theraspid reptiles. This is *Megazostrodon*, about the size and weight of a shrew.

Left

The tiny Dawn Horse, *Eohippus* lived in jungle surroundings, where it could hide from enemies. It is browsing off the soft leaves. Notice the separate toes for walking on soft ground. It is an ancestor of all horses, and lived during the Eocene Period.

Right

Modern breeds of horses vary from little ponies to the large shire horses. The genuine wild ancestor still lives in Mongolia. Apart from this there are also wild asses and zebras. There are also a number of so-called wild horses running loose. In parts of America these are the mustangs which have escaped. In Britain there are wild ponies in places like Scotland, Wales, Ireland, Dartmoor and Exmoor, usually in mountains or on moorland and heaths.

Below

This theraspid or mammal-like reptile is called *Thrinaxodon*. About 50 cm (18 in) long it stood upright like a true mammal, with its body well off the ground. It was probably warm-blooded.

Sabre-tooths were large and fierce pre-historic cats with very long canine teeth. These were used like daggers for stabbing their prey so that they could feed on blood. They even hunted our ancestors. This one is *Smilodon* (smy-low-don) found in North America. Many sabre-tooths were trapped in the tar-pits at Rancho la Brea in California.

Left

This splendid giant, called *Megaceros* (meg-ass-er-oss) is the largest deer which ever lived. Also called the Irish deer its remains have often been found complete in Irish peat bogs, buried in the peat. It lived during the Ice Age and was hunted by Stone-age man. It stood 1½ m (5 ft) at the shoulders, and had antlers up to 4 m (13 ft) across.

Below

Just like horses many fossil elephants have been discovered. They, too, started very small and ended up as giants. The tusks of this Deinotherium evolved from the front teeth of the lower jaw. They were probably used for grubbing up roots.

Above

The modern sloth is descended from a prehistoric mammal called *Megatherium* and lives in trees in South America. It moves very slowly and is well hidden as tiny green plants grow on its hair.

This is one of the many large mammals which roamed the countryside during the Eocene Period. Called *Uintatherium* (yew-in-ta-theer-i-um) it was about 4 m (13 ft) long, and looked like a huge rhinoceros with horns and tusks.

Far right
The well-known Woolly Mammoth, *Mammuthus* (mam-oo-thus) lived during the Ice Age, and wandered in herds through the bitter countryside of Europe, north Asia and North America over 10,000 years ago. Frozen bodies found in the Far North, where the ground never melts, have been found in a kind of 'deep-freeze'. Also the bones of some 50 thousand mammoths have been found in Siberia, and many thousands more in Europe and North America. This model is very accurate, even to the colour of the thick coat of hair. Mammoths were hunted by prehistoric man, who ate the flesh and used the tusks to make ornaments and tools. Paintings on the cave walls of the Stone-age artists show that this elephant had a hump on its back, likely a store of food in the form of fat.

Below right
The Woolly Rhinoceros, *Coelodonta* (see-low-don-ta) is another Ice Age mammal, well protected with a thick coat. It, too, was hunted by driving it into traps. Like the Mammoth frozen bodies have been found in the Far North. It was a little smaller than the modern rhino, and measured 1½ m (5 ft). The remains of such giants were known to the ancient Greeks who thought they were the remains of the one-eyed Cyclops.

Below
The Giant Armadillo, *Glyptodon* (glip-tow-don) was covered with a hard, bony skin, rather like the shell of a tortoise. It was 3½ m (10 ft) long and used its clawed feet for digging up food. It had powerful jaws and crushing teeth for eating plants.

As mammals were evolving and taking over the earth, life underwater was also changing – but at a much slower rate. Many of the fish of Eocene times are still with us today, such as the sharks and rays shown in this picture. At the same times, groups of fishes were adapting themselves to different underwater conditions which is why species that are today found in some seas would not be found elsewhere.

Left
This strange looking Australian mammal the *Platypus*, meaning 'flat-feet' lives along the banks of streams and lakes in eastern parts of Australia. It swims well and can also burrow in the bankside where it has a nest, and where its eggs are laid. It is a true 'living fossil' from the days when mammals were evolving from reptiles. So is the Echidna or Spiny Anteater, the only other modern egg-laying mammal.

ACKNOWLEDGEMENTS

The publishers would like to thank the following organisations and individuals for their kind permission to reproduce the pictures in this book:

Heather Angel: 12, 15 above, 26 above, 29 above. Ardea; 17, 83 above; (P. Green) 4–5, 7, 18 above, 20 above, 23; (A. Hayward) Endpapers, 1, 63, 69, 72–3 above; (J. Mason) 11. British Museum (Natural History): (Imitor) 8, 10 above, 20 below, 21 above, 25, 26 below, 27, 29 below, 30 above, 32 left, 33 below, 35, 37, 38, 39, 41, 42–3, 43, 48–9, 55, 56–7, 61, 65, 72–3 below, 76 below, 77, 79, 82, 83 below, 87 below, 90, 92–3; (Photoresources) 21 below. Gene Cox: 33 above. Bruce Coleman: 93; (J. Burton) 16 below, 44; (E. Crichton) 14 above; (F. Erize) 87 above; (Wernerstoy) 16 above. European Colour Library: 30 below, 52–3. Alan Hutchison Library: (A. Howland) 15 below. Horniman Museum, London: (Photoresources) 64. Institute of Geological Sciences: 13 above, 24–5. A. Leutscher: 45, 47. Natural Science Photos: (F. Greenway) 36–7, 46–7; (A. Hayward) 2–3, 28, 31, 32 right, 16, 40, 49, 51, 58–9, 62–3, 66–7, 68, 70–1, 75, 78; (G. Kinns) 62, 84–5, 86, 88–9, 91; (P. Ward) 17, 36, 54. Novosti Press Agency: 10 below. Rida Photographic Library: (D. Bayliss) 13 below. Zefa: (R. Everts) 18 below; (Hemlinger) 9; (Ludens) 76 above; (H. Steenmaus) 14 below. Zoological Society of London: 81.

Picture research: Anne Williams